Introduction

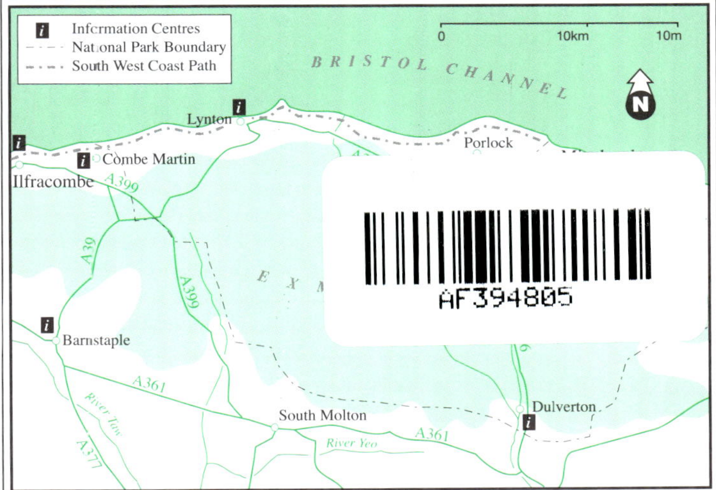

Exmoor sits just south of the Bristol Channel, straddling the border of Somerset and Devon. The name is derived from the area of grass and heather moorland surrounding the upper waters of the River Exe, but the definition has now been extended to include lower level farmland and woodland, as well as the area's spectacular coastal scenery. There have been a number of historic delineations of the area – going back to the boundaries of the royal hunting forest – but for the purpose of this book we will be using the boundary of the Exmoor National Park (*see* map), which was created in 1954.

This is an area of low population in small towns and scattered villages. The major settlements are just outside the boundary: Minehead *(3)*, Ilfracombe and Barnstaple. These are the main service centres for the area, though you will also find information and good shopping in the largest towns within the National Park: Porlock and Lynton/ Lynmouth *(12,13,14)* in the north and Dulverton *(20)* in the south. It should be added that the towns and villages within the Park are varied and picturesque, with winding main streets, fine architecture and numerous thatched buildings. The little village of Dunster *(1,2)* is a particular gem, with its hill-top castle and old yarn market.

The area covered by the National Park is quite modest – approximately 30 miles/48kms from east to west at its widest

Dunster Castle (Walk 1)

point, and 15 miles/25kms from north to south – but it feels larger than it is. This is partly because of the great variety of landscape; partly because of the nature of the roads. Please note that ample time should be left for any journey. Even the main roads through the area (the A39, A396 and A399) are winding, and once on the minor roads navigation can be tricky. Make sure you have a good map or navigation device.

Not all of the National Park is open for walkers, but there are large areas of access land and numerous rights of way, plus a number of waymarked trails (*see* OS map OL9 for details).

The greatest density of walks in this guide is along the coast, which contains the bulk of the area's most dramatic scenery and a continuous footpath (the South West Coast Path: *see* end of Intro). At the east end of the area is the handsome resort of Minehead, with the steep-sided mound of North Hill/Bossington Hill behind the coast to the west. There are numerous paths through the steep woodland at the east end of the hill *(3)*, and fine walking over the open moorland and mature woodland beyond *(4,5)*. The hill ends at the low ground behind Porlock Bay, with its splendid shingle bank *(6)*. West from Porlock Weir *(8)* the coast is backed by cliffs and steep wooded banks as far as Combe Martin. This guide contains a description of the well-known walk west from the little harbour of Lynmouth to the dramatic crags of the Valley of Rocks *(14)*, as well as a section of the SWCP running across the steep slopes between Heddon's Mouth and Woody Bay *(15,16)*.

Behind the coast a number of valleys wind into the higher ground. The best known – and most dramatic – of these is the wooded gorge

carrying the East Lyn River east from Lynmouth. There are fine walks
up the gorge to the old tearooms at Watersmeet *(12,13)*. Elsewhere,
the finest oak woodland in the area is in the valley of the Horner
Water *(7)*, while the valley of the Badgworthy Water – which leads
the walker through woodland and out on to the open moor *(10,11)* – is
famous as the backdrop for R D Blackmore's novel *Lorna Doone*. At
the far east of the area the tributaries of the River Avill lead into the
woods south of Dunster and climb to the ancient settlement of Bat's
Castle *(1)*.

The largest body of freshwater in the area is the man-made Wimbleball Lake, in the farmland of the south-east. There is a path around
the reservoir *(18)* and another walk over the moorland of Haddon Hill
to the south, then back by the handsome wooded valley of the River
Haddeo *(19)*. There are further wooded valley walks from Dulverton
(20) and Withypool *(9)* – the latter leading to Tarr Steps. This is one
of Exmoor's most distinctive man-made features: a clapper bridge
which, according to some theories, dates back 3,000 years.

The South West Coast Path

There are a number of waymarked trails through Exmoor, but the
longest and most popular is the South West Coast Path. This is
England's longest waymarked trail and runs 630 miles/1,014kms
around the coast, starting at Minehead in Somerset, then continuing
around Devon and Cornwall before ending at Poole in Dorset. This
guide contains seven short walks which include parts of the SWCP.
Two other guides in the
series continue around
the coast in the same
fashion, describing short
walks branching off from
the main route. If you
are interested in walking
the entire path and wish
further information, visit
**www.southwestcoast-
path.org.uk**.

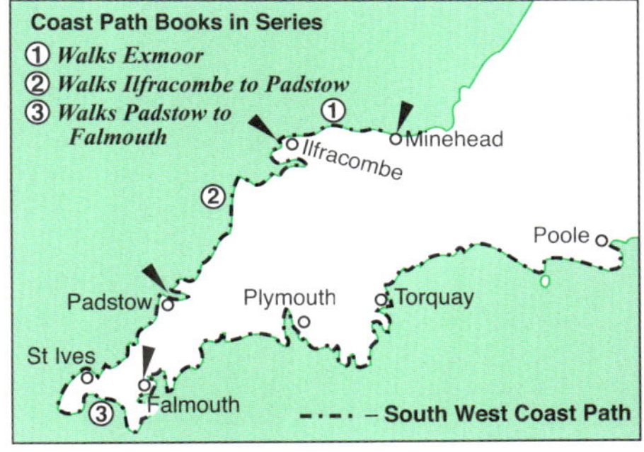

1 **Deer Park Circuit /**
2 **Conygar Wood Circuit** _____________ **B/C**

1) *A moderate circuit through woods and open ground, passing a fine old bridge and leading to two Iron Age hill forts which provide a good viewpoint. Length:* **3 miles/5km**; *Height Climbed:* **520ft/160m**. **2)** *A short climb to a hilltop folly offering fine views. Length:* **1 mile/1.6km**; *Height Climbed:* **160ft/50m**.

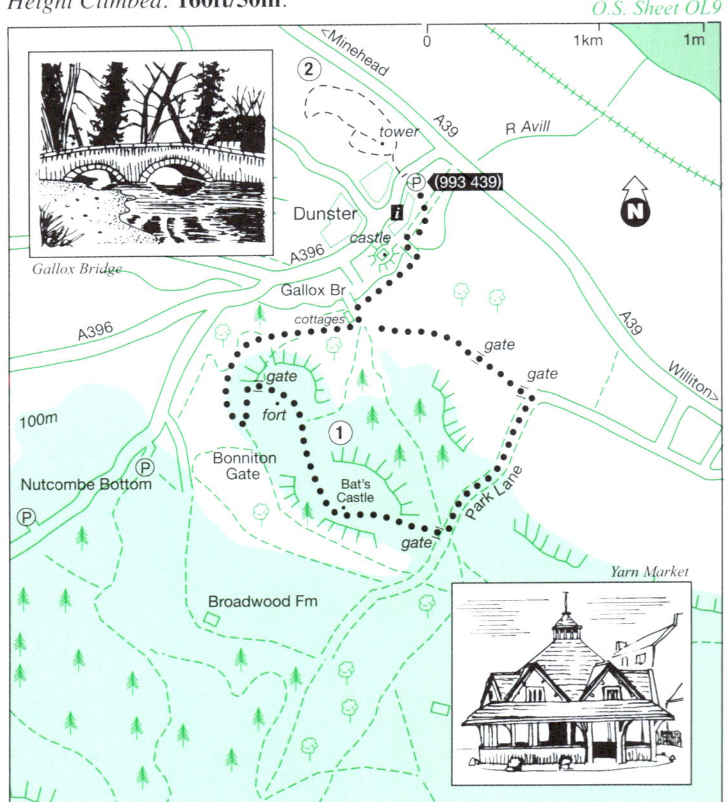

The village of Dunster, just east of Minehead on the A39, is worth a visit on its own account. Its castle (National Trust), winding streets and old Yarn Market make it one of the major attractions of the area. It is also a terrific centre for walking.

There are a number of potential routes in the area. A modest circuit through Dunster Wood is outlined below, along with a second, shorter route to the north of the village. For those looking for further walks, the 1:25,000 OS map shows the full range of paths available.

Walk 1) Park in the car park to the left of the road as you enter the village from the A39. Go through the pedestrian gate at the top-left corner of the car park and walk straight ahead, up a slope, to reach a sign-post. Go straight ahead here (Gallox Bridge).

Walk straight down the slope beyond, pass through two gates in line, cross an access road and contin-ue, roughly shadowing a fence (the boundary fence for the castle) to your right. This leads you to the corner of the field with a bridge over the River Avill visible beyond.

Cross the bridge and follow the riverside path beyond to reach Gallox Bridge – a narrow, two-arched pack-horse bridge.

Turn left on the near side, walking past a terrace of thatched cottages to reach a complex junction. Go ahead-right at this junction and climb across a wooded slope on a good track.

At the next junction keep right (marked by a blue-tipped bridleway sign). Continue on the bridleway until, at a junction, a footpath sign for 'Bonniton Gate' points off to the left. Turn on to this path. At the next junction double back to the left on a path which climbs to a gate in a deer fence.

The path beyond leads you out of the trees and on to the open ridge. Pass to the left of the grassy ring of the first Iron Age fort then dip and climb again to pass through the mid-dle of the second fort: Bat's Castle.

Descend beyond, along the ridge, until you reach a signposted junction just before a gate in a fence. A path to Dunster heads left at this point, but for this route go through the gate and turn left down the shaded old roadway of Park Lane.

When the lane turns hard right you go left (Dunster), into a grazing area. Walk straight down the pathless field beyond to reach a gate then follow the path beyond back to the first junction.

Walk 2) Walk out of the car park and turn left along the road, towards the village. After a short distance there is a sign pointing right for Conygar Wood. Follow that uphill, between hedges, to reach a gate on the edge of the wood.

Immediately beyond the gate there is a T-junction. Go right (Conygar Circuit) and follow the green markers round the hill. At the back of the hill there is a junction, and a short detour to the left leads on to Conygar Tower – a tall, cylindrical folly built in 1775.

Having enjoyed the view, double back to the junction and turn first left to return to the start.

A circuit, steep in places, across the slope of the coast north of Mine-head. There is a dense network of paths in the area, making navigation tricky in places but also providing shortcuts. The paths pass through fine woodland and open country and there are good coast views.
Length: **4½ miles/7km**; *Height Climbed:* **820ft/250m**.

O.S. Sheet OL9

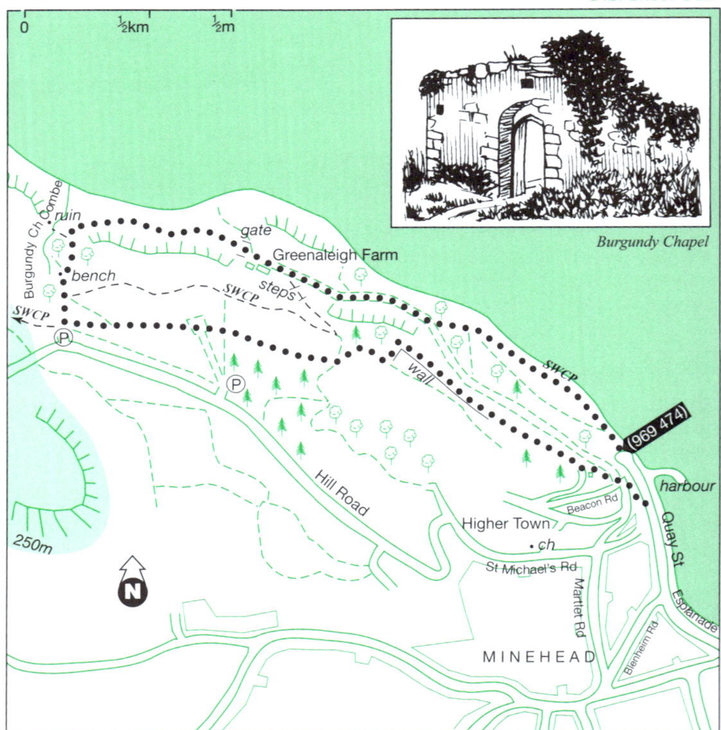

Burgundy Chapel

This walk is described as if started from Minehead. It is also possible to start it from a car park on Hill Road (*see* map). If you are doing this, follow the driving instructions for Walk 4 until you have left the houses behind. The road starts along the ridge with a wood to the right. Park in the first car park to the right after the end of the trees.

If starting from Minehead, walk/drive north along the Esplanade/Quay St. The road passes the little harbour and ends at a turning point just beyond. Take the right-hand path from the end of the road: the start of the South West Coast Path.

The clear path runs behind the beach in a flat, grassy area used by dog-owners. At the end of the flat area the path enters trees and climbs away from the shingle beach. After a short distance you reach a signposted junction with a path going back-left to Minehead. This is the first of three similar junctions on this stretch of the path: follow the signs for the Coastal Path (marked by an acorn symbol) and Greenaleigh.

After the third junction you are on a metalled driveway. Ignore a path heading right, to the beach, and continue through the fields approaching Greenaleigh Farm. Just before the buildings there is a split, with the Coastal Path heading left, up steps. If you wish to avoid the steepest climb, go left (*see* map); otherwise, keep straight on (Burgundy Chapel).

Walk past the buildings, ignore a path heading right (Greenaleigh Beach) and go through a gate. Beyond, you run across the slope near the bottom of a wooded area.

The path reaches Burgundy Chapel Combe, turns left and starts to climb up the narrow valley. Watch for a path heading right, down steps. This leads across the stream to the remains of the medieval chapel. Return to the main path and continue climbing.

You reach a bench and a path heads right. Keep left, climbing with the valley to your right. At a junction keep straight on (North Hill) to reach the junction just below the car park on Hill Road. Go back-left (Minehead seafront).

Follow a clear track across the open slope, slightly downhill. You cross a concrete square and a track heads off ahead-right. Ignore this and keep straight on, quickly reaching another junction in a line of trees. Keep straight on (Minehead).

From this point, attempts at detailed description are pointless: a mass of paths runs through the woodland ahead and not all the junctions are signposted. Where they are, follow the signs for Minehead and you should end up walking along an increasingly clear track at the top of the wood, with a wall to your right. (Don't worry if you are not; just keep walking in roughly the correct direction and you are bound to reach some part of Minehead.)

If you are on the top path, you pass two posts set into the track, just before it joins the public road. Go ahead-left (Minehead) and zig-zag down the wooded slope to reach a hairpin bend on a metalled road (Beacon Road). Take the path marked by a yellow arrow and continue zig-zagging downhill, eventually running between houses. Keep taking the downhill option at junctions and you will eventually end up back on Quay St.

*A moderate circuit, steep in places, mostly through mixed woodland. Passes some beautiful thatched cottages and a fine old church. Paths generally good and fine views from the start point. Length: **3¹/₂ miles/ 5.6km**; Height Climbed: **490ft/150m**. Possible link with Walk 5.*

O.S. Sheet OL9

To reach the start of this route (and of Walk 5) you need to find your way onto Hill Road – the single-track road running west along the open ridge to the west of Higher Town, at the north end of Minehead. One route is by Blenheim Road, Martlet Road and St Michael's Road, but there are links from other parts of the town. Alternatively, if you are having a long walking day, you can get there on foot starting along Walk 3 then continuing along the Coastal Path. It is about 6 miles/9.6km from the start of Walk 3 to the start of this route.

At the west end of Hill Road

there is a turning area and a car park. As you enter the turning area a path heads off back-left, signed for the Easy Access Trail. Follow this clear path through mixed woodland, roughly parallel to the road, until you reach the handsome sandstone block of the 'Wind and Weather Hut' – a Victorian shelter.

Walk straight up to the road beyond this and turn right. Immediately, a sign points right for the bridleway to Selworthy. Walk round a wooden barrier and follow the grassy track beyond.

Ignore the path going right to Bury Castle and continue; initially with moorland to the left and trees to the right, then through trees with a small stream to your right.

The stream approaches a junction with a second stream in Selworthy Combe. Just before the confluence the track goes right, over the first stream, then crosses the next stream to reach a junction with another track. Go right (Selworthy) and follow the combe down towards the village.

Just before the village is reached a wall climbs up to join the track and a path drops down to the right to reach a footbridge. A sign points right for Bossington. This will be your onward route, but for now make a detour downhill to visit the splendid thatched cottages of Selworthy Green and the whitewashed Church of All Saints.

Double back to the junction (there are also path links from Selworthy (*see* map) and take the Bossington path, over the footbridge and through a gate. Beyond this you are in dense woodland on a steep slope. (There is a mass of paths through this wood and there is a good chance you will miss one of the turns. If you do, just remember that the car park is at the top of the hill: keep climbing and you won't go far wrong).

The path forks immediately. Go left to reach a signposted junction. Keep straight on here (Bossington). At the next junction, just beyond, keep straight on again (Bossington).

Keep straight on at the next junction and continue to join a clearer track at a four-way junction. Go ahead-left (Bossington). You should now be running along the edge of the wood with fields down to your left.

The next fork is by St Katherine's Well (a pile of stones and a spring to the right of the track). There is no sign, but keep left. The fields end to the left and the track turns right, into Holnicote Combe. In the heart of the combe there is a four-way junction. Keep straight on (Bossington).

At the next junction a track comes up from behind-left and climbs ahead-right, signed for Bossington Hill. Follow this track, up and across the wooded slope. You climb to join a clear track contouring across the slope. Go left along this.

You pass a wooden hut before reaching a further four-way junction. Go ahead-right, eventually climbing to a gate at the top of the wood. Walk straight on across the open ground (Selworthy Beacon) to return to the car park at the top of the slope.

5 Bossington Hill & Lynch Combe ———— B

*A circuit on clear tracks and paths over open ground, giving terrific coastal views. Length: **3¹/₂ miles/5.6km**; Height Climbed: **460ft/140m**. Possible links with Walks 4 & 6.*

To reach the start of this walk, follow the instructions for Walk 4 and turn right into the car park.

From the end of the car park nearest Minehead a clear track sets off, signed for Bossington Hill. Start along this, ignoring a track heading off to the left. A little further on a path heads left, down the slope. Ignore this and stick to the main track, through gorse and heather.

The track begins to swing left and another track comes in from behind-right. Keep left. A short distance beyond you join a second track, this one marked by the acorn symbol of the Coastal Path. Keep left again. After 50 paces there is a further junction. The left-hand track is your return route; for now go ahead-right (Coastal Path).

Follow this clear track, with the cairn on Bossington Hill visible to your left, and the village of Porlock below. Keep left at two signposted forks and continue to reach a multiple junction at the head of a combe.

The path ahead (Porlock), down the combe, links with Walk 6. For this route go ahead-left (Lynch Combe). The path contours round the steep slope of Bossington Hill, giving fine views of Porlock and the cliffs and moors beyond.

Follow the path through the little valley of Church Combe then into

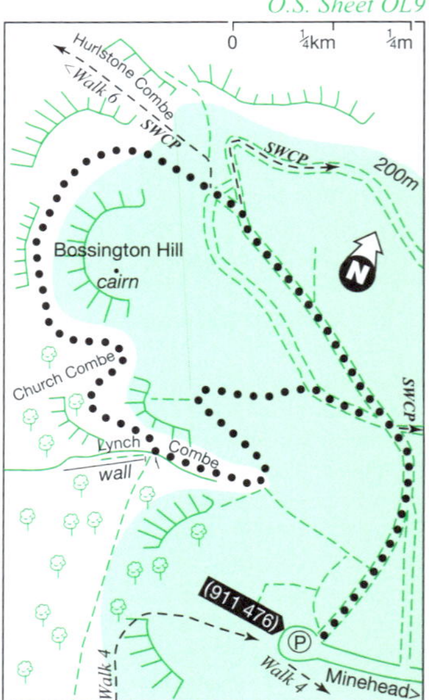

woodland and on into the heart of Lynch Combe. Here there is a wall, with a signposted junction on the near side. Go left here (Minehead) and climb up the combe with a little stream to your right.

Climb out of the trees and you reach a junction. Go left (Selworthy Beacon) and climb to the ridge at the edge of the combe. Here there is a further junction. Go right (bridleway) and keep right at a subsequent junction to return to the original track.

*A short circuit on good paths, through woodland and open ground, to a rocky headland and shingle beach. Length: **2 miles/3.2km**; Height Climbed: **260ft/80m**. Possible link with Walk 5.*

To reach this walk, drive 4 miles west from Minehead on the A39 then turn north onto the road to Bossington. Drive down to this picturesque little village and park in the car park.

Look for the sign for the path to Hurlstone and walk out of the car park; crossing a footbridge over the river and turning left at the junction beyond. The path starts by the river then pulls away to the right, running along the foot of a wooded slope with fields to the left. Looking ahead you can see the shingle bank which protects the fields.

When the trees end the path edges right, through a gate, and continues, now climbing, with a slope of bracken and gorse to the right. You reach a junction by a National Trust cairn. To link with Walk 5 turn right (Minehead), but for this walk keep straight on.

After a short distance there is a split. A short detour to the left leads down to the shingle beach – a dramatic sight but difficult to walk on. Otherwise go ahead-right. After a short distance a path heads off back-right. This is your return route, but for now continue climbing to the remains of the old coastguard station on Hurlstone Point.

The path continues beyond the ruin, but it is narrow and steep and should not be attempted in bad condi-

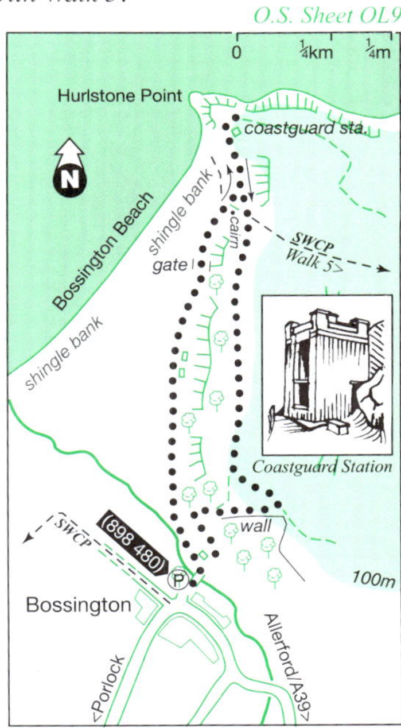

tions. For this walk, double back to the junction and keep left.

Follow this clear path, contouring across the slope, until a large wall climbs the slope to your right with a wood beyond it. Turn right at the junction on the near side of the wall (Bossington) and follow the rough path downhill; passing through a gate then continuing through trees to return to the footbridge by the car park.

7 Horner Woods   A

A circuit on rough paths, starting with a steep climb onto open moor-land and returning on a riverside path through fine oak woodland. A National Park leaflet is available. Length: **6 miles/9.6km**; *Height Climbed:* **790ft/240m**.

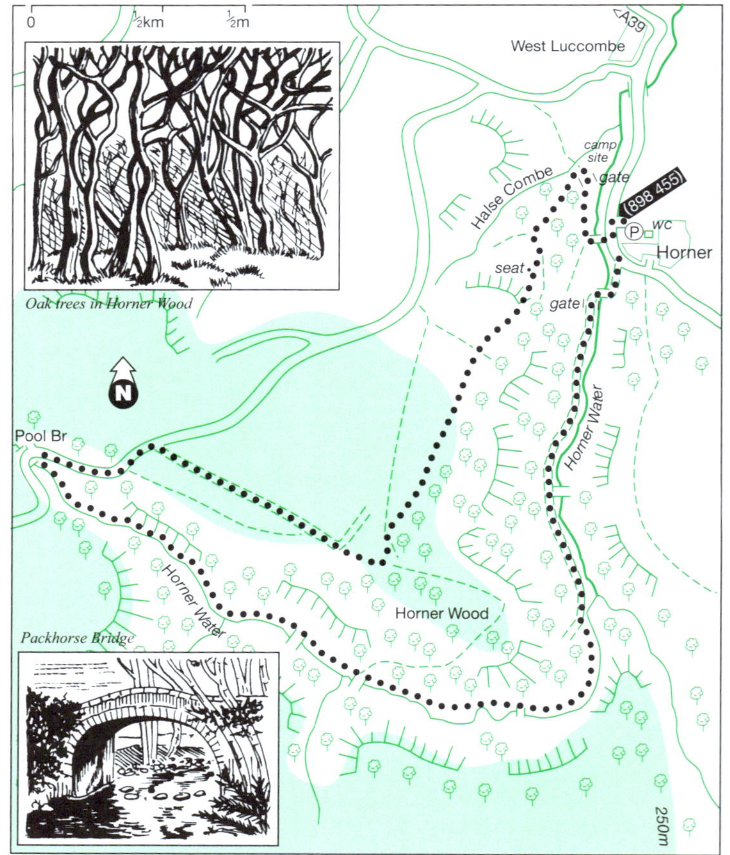

Oak trees in Horner Wood

Packhorse Bridge

To reach the start of this walk, turn south off the A39 just east of Porlock, at the sign for West Luccombe. Keep straight on at the junction in the little village to reach the village of Horner (about a mile off the A39). Park in the car park to the left of the road.

Walk back out on to the road and turn left. After 30 paces there is a sign pointing right for a path to Porlock. Follow this path over a hump-backed packhorse bridge over Horner Water and turn right. Immediately there is a signposted junction: keep straight on, climbing slightly away from the stream.

The path runs round the bottom of the slope through trees before turning left and going through a gate, just before crossing the little stream in Halse Combe. Turn left on the near side of the stream, climbing straight up the hill with the stream down to your right; through woodland at first, then along an open ridge.

Climb to a signposted junction with Granny's Ride and turn left. After about 80 paces there is a split. This time go ahead-right (Pentley Seat) and follow a rough, clear path up to the seat. This is a fine viewpoint, with good views north to Bossington, Allerford and Selworthy along the foot of Bossington Hill (*see* Walks 4, 5 & 6)

Continue on the clear path beyond the seat, still climbing and roughly shadowing the top of Horner Wood to your left. A grassy track crosses the way. Keep straight on. Then the trees come up from the left and, just

as you join them, a path comes in from behind-right (marked by a post). Keep straight on here, and right at the fork just beyond, continuing to the right of the wood.

You stop climbing and start to descend, with the path now passing through a fringe of trees at the top of the wood. In a few paces, when the path begins to edge further into the wood, keep straight on along a fainter path beside the trees. In a very short distance you reach a T-junction with a clear path. Turn right along this.

In 200 paces a track comes in from the right and runs on ahead. Keep straight on along this and follow it across the moor to join a quiet public road.

Turn left and follow this road (keeping out of the way of any traffic on the steep hill) down into the trees, then on downhill to hump-backed Pool Bridge. Turn left on the near side of the bridge (Horner). You are now in the west end of Horner Wood: an extensive, ancient oak wood which is very rich in lichens and mosses and also houses a significant population of red deer.

There are still $2^1/_2$ miles/4km of the walk to go, but the route now becomes easy to follow. Just stick to the clear, rough path down the left-hand side of Horner Water, ignoring occasional footbridges to your right.

Near the edge of the village you go through a gate, cross a stone bridge, then follow the track beyond back to the public road in Horner. Turn left to return to the start.

 Porlock Weir to Culbone Church ___________ **B**

A walk on clear footpaths through coastal woodland and along quiet public roads, passing a fine old church. Length: **5¹/₂ miles/8.8km**; *Height Climbed:* **950ft/290m**.

O.S. Sheet OL9

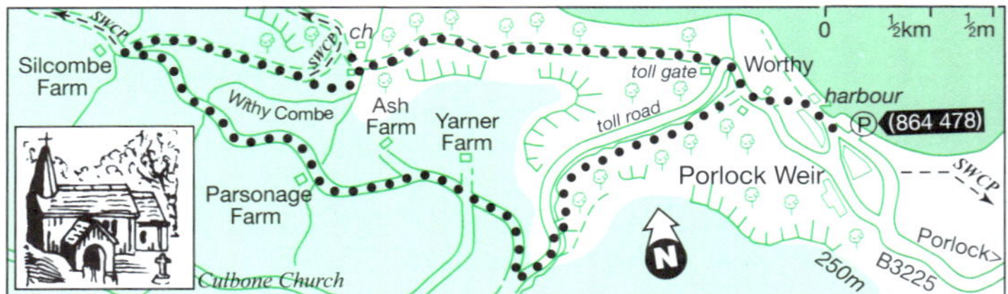

Park in the car park by the harbour at Porlock Weir, 2 miles west of Porlock on the B3225. Walk straight on, past the harbour, to reach a signposted junction. Go left (Culbone), climbing a flight of steps to reach a kissing-gate leading into a field.

Go through the gate and turn right beyond. Follow the field edge through two fields to join an access track at a hairpin bend. Go ahead-left and follow the track up to the road.

Continue along the road. Just past Worthy Manor a track goes left, into the trees. That is your return route, but for now keep straight on to reach an extraordinary double archway at the foot of the Worthy Toll Road. Go through the right-hand arch.

The next mile/1.6km is difficult to describe but easy to follow: just follow the path signed for Culbone/ Coast Path at each junction, across and up (in a series of zig-zags) the wooded slope until the path peaks and descends into Withy Combe.

Cross a bridge over the stream to reach St Bueno's: a tiny parish church dating from at least the 13th century. At the bottom of the churchyard there is a gate. Go through this and turn right (Silcombe Farm).

A rough path follows the stream back under the track then climbs on beyond, gradually climbing the slope to the right to join the line of the Coast Path. Go left along this.

Follow this clear track up to the public road. Turn left (ie, away from Silcombe Farm). The road is a dead-end, and so quiet, but it is still narrow and care must be taken with any traffic.

Follow this road for a mile/1.6km, enjoying the views, to reach a junction by the entrance to Yarner Farm. Keep straight on (Toll Road).

The road descends to a hairpin at the bottom of a combe. Stick to the road for a little further until a sign points right for the path to Porlock Weir. Go through a gate, cross the stream and keep left at the junction beyond (Worthy Combe), then follow the track shadowing the toll road back down to the public road at Worthy.

9 Withypool & Tarr Steps —————————————— A

A fine riverside path through woodland to a splendid old stone bridge. The path is rough in places and can be slippery after rain. Length: **9 miles/14.4km** (there and back); *Height Climbed:* **560ft/170m**.

Park in the car park at the west end of the village of Withypool – 9 miles north-west of Dulverton (*see* Walk 20) on the B3223 and a minor road.

Walk back out of the car park and turn left; over the bridge, past the inn and up the slope beyond the village. After a short distance there is a stile to the right of the road and a sign for the path to Tarr Steps.

This is a very pleasant riverside walk through woods and fields. There are numerous gates and junctions but there is no doubt about the route: just stick to the path to the left of the river and follow it down to the ford and ancient clapper bridge by Tarr Farm Inn.

The easiest return is by the same route. For an alternative, cross the bridge, walk a few paces along the road then head half-right up a metalled track (Withypool Hill). When the track goes into a house go ahead-right on a path marked by a post with a blue top.

Climb to a gate and beyond it turn right, still with a wall to your right, along the bottom of a narrow field. At the corner turn left, up the side of the field (blue arrow). Go through a further gate and keep straight on, now with a fence to your left, through two further fields.

At the end of the field, with the roofs of Parsonage Farm visible

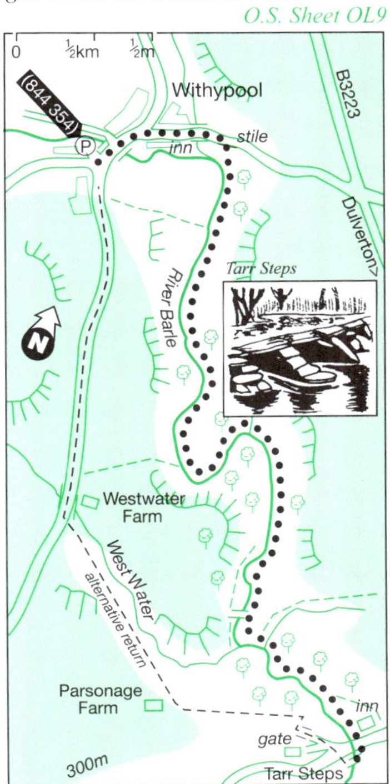

ahead, turn right along the side of the field. Keep straight on through five fields to join the public road just to the left of Westwater Farm.

Turn right and follow this quiet road, with verges for most of the way, for 2 miles/3.2km; along the edge of Withypool Hill and back to the start.

Walks Exmoor

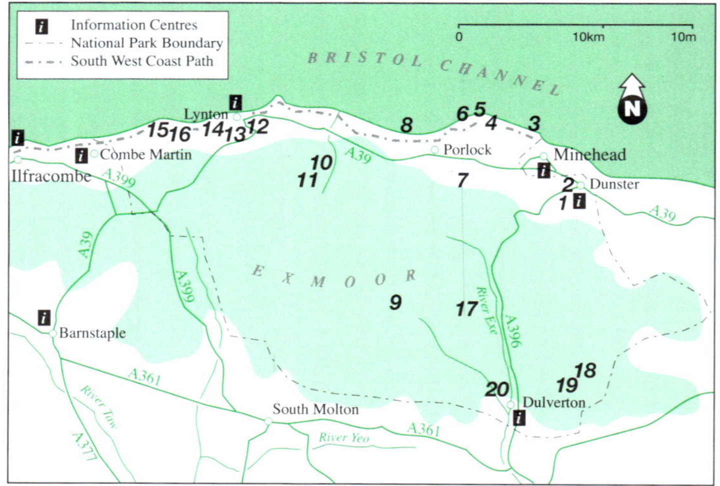

Grades

A ...... Full walking equipment required. Underfoot conditions occasionally wet or rough and some navigation may be needed.

B ...... Strong walking footwear and waterproof clothing required. Underfoot conditions generally good and navigation largely straightforward.

C ...... Comfortable walking footwear recommended.

—www.pocketwalks.com—

Published by: *Hallewell Publications, Scotland*
Printed by: *Barr Printers, Glenrothes*

Walks Exmoor

10 **Malmsmead & Oare** / 11 **Doone Valley**_______ **B/A**

Two walks starting up the valley associated with the novel Lorna Doone.
10) *A short loop, returning through farmland and past a fine old church.
Take care: grazing animals. Length:* **3 miles/4.8km**; *Height Climbed:*
230ft/70m. **11)** *A longer walk with a return across moorland. Some
navigation needed. Length:* **7 miles/11.2km**; *Height Climbed:* **660ft/
200m**.

These two walks start from the car
park at the hamlet of Malmsmead. To
reach it, drive 5 miles east from Lynmouth on the A39 and turn right at the
sign for Lorna Doone Farm. Follow
the minor road to a junction at Oare
and turn right to reach the car park.
As the name will suggest, this area is
associated with R D Blackmore's *Lorna Doone* (1869) – the most famous
novel associated with Exmoor.

Walks 10 & 11) Walk out of the
car park and turn left. You quickly
reach the road junction by the bridge
over Badgworthy Water. Keep
straight on up the narrow public road.
After a short climb the road begins to
turn to the right. Just before it does
so there is a gate to the left and a sign
for the bridleway to Badgworthy Valley. Go through the gate and continue
along a clear track.

Ignoring field entrances, follow
this track until the lane ends at two
gates. Go through the right-hand gate
and continue on a rough track at the
bottom of a field. This leads you to a
second gate. Continue beyond this to
reach the footbridge leading over the
river to Cloud Farm.

Walk 10) For the shorter walk,
cross the bridge (Oare Church) and
walk up towards the near end of the
farm house (and tearoom), to reach

the next sign. Edge left here (Oare Church), passing through a gate and continuing up a clear track. Ignore a path which quickly heads off left and continue climbing up and across the slope.

Pass through a gate in a wall (yellow square) and continue climbing, now in an open grazing field. Go through a gate at the top of the field and continue. A tongue of trees appears ahead, in a combe climbing up from the left. Follow the clear track round the edge of the trees. On the far side of the trees the track swings right. When this happens keep straight on, along a fainter path by a fence, to reach a gate. Go through this and continue down the left-hand side of two fields to reach the road.

Turn left, past the handsome 15th-century church, then turn right at a junction. The road crosses a bridge and edges left. Opposite a farm entrance there is a gate to the left of the road and a sign for the bridleway to Malmsmead.

Follow a clear path past some trees by the Oare Water. When the trees end you enter a field. Aim to pass to the right of the farm buildings ahead then continue to reach a signposted junction. Go left (Malmsmead), cross a footbridge, climb to the public road and turn right to return to the start.

Walk 11) For the longer walk, continue up the right-hand side of the river (Doone Valley) on a clear path. After a short distance you pass a memorial to R D Blackmore, beyond which the path passes through fine oak woodland by the riverside.

Ignore paths to right and left and continue by the river for a mile/1.6km, until the trees end.

The path now climbs across a slope of grass and bracken towards the edge of a tributary valley – Hoccombe Combe – before edging right, into the combe, and reaching a signposted junction amongst some moss-covered walls (the remains of a medieval village). Go straight on here (Brendon Common).

Follow the faint path through the old walls and out on to the moor. When the last wall pulls away to the left keep straight on. The rough path fords a stream then climbs to a gate in a wall, visible on the horizon.

Beyond the gate there are paths in all directions. Keep straight on and, within a mile/1.6km, the way becomes clearer and descends to Lankcombe Ford.

Beyond the ford there are three paths climbing the far slope. Take the clear one heading ahead-right and climb to a signposted junction with a clear track. Turn right (Malmsmead).

Follow this track for $\frac{1}{2}$ mile/ 0.8km, until it begins to edge to the right. At this point a grassy path heads off to the left (post). It splits almost immediately. The right-hand path heads up Malmsmead Hill, but for this route keep to the left.

Follow this path to a ford then keep straight on along a clear track (ignoring one coming in from the right at one point) to reach the public road. Turn right along this (taking care as the road narrows) to return to the start.

12 Watersmeet / 13 Watersmeet & The Cleaves _ C/B

Two walks starting up the deep, wooded valley behind Lynmouth and passing the old Tea Gardens at Watersmeet. **12)** *A moderate walk, up the valley and back again.* Length: **4 miles/6.4km**; Height Climbed: **330ft/100m** (undulating). **13)** *A longer version, with steep climbs and descents and wonderful views.* Length: **5 miles/8km**; Height Climbed: **820ft/250m**.

The walk up the deep, wooded valley of the East Lyn River from Lynmouth to the old Tea Gardens at Watersmeet House is one of the classic Exmoor walks. Here are two variations on the route.

Walks 12 & 13) Starting from Lynmouth (there is also a car park above Watersmeet on the A39 – *see map*), find the car park by the A39 road bridge, with the National Park Information Centre in one corner, and start walking up the right-hand side of the river.

Follow the clear path to the second footbridge crossing the river. Cross this and continue up the far side. You are now in a narrow, wooded valley with the river running over rapids to your right.

Follow the riverside path until it climbs a little and forks. Go left here (Woodland Walk). At the next fork keep left again (Woodland Walk) and follow a fine, woodland path across the wooded slope.

A little under a mile from the first fork you reach a signposted junction in Chisel Combe. Keep straight on here (Watersmeet) and follow the path back down to the river. Walk past the end of the elegant, single-span Chiselcombe Bridge and continue to reach Watersmeet: a 19th-century fishing lodge (now owned by the National Trust) at a wonderful spot by the confluence of two rivers. They have been serving teas here for over 100 years.

Possible extension paths continue up both rivers, but for these routes cross the two footbridges beyond the lodge to reach the far side of the valley.

Walk 12) For the shorter route, follow the path down the far side of the river, eventually recrossing to reach the original fork in the path. Retrace your steps to the start.

Walk 13) For the longer route, walk a short way down the far side then double back at a junction. After a short climb you reach a further junction. Go right here (Lynton via Cleaves).

Climb the steep slope to reach the staff car park (just down the road from the visitor car park). Cross the road (carefully) and start climbing up and across the wooded slope on a path signed for Lynmouth.

At the top of the wood there is a grassy area and a sign for an Iron Age Enclosure. Walk straight across the ring. Looking ahead you can see a path climbing in a gap between trees. That is your route: climb up above the trees and turn right, quickly joining another path at a signposted junction. Go ahead-right (Lynmouth).

This is a fine path, with excellent views over the wooded valley and down to Lynmouth. After $^1/_2$ mile/ 0.8km it zig-zags down one side of a small combe then up the other. At the next signposted junction keep straight on (Lynmouth), then at the next one go right (Lynmouth). It looks as though you are walking along a short grassy promontory and then in to thin air, but a rough path starts down and across the steep, wooded slope.

There is one signposted junction (keep straight on), but apart from that there is no doubt about the route; descending steeply, sometimes in zig-zags, to the edge of Lynmouth.

The final descent into the village is on a steep, metalled lane (slippery when wet) between houses.

14 The Valley of Rocks
B

A short, steep, classic coast walk leading to a dramatic rocky valley. The paths are good but care must be taken on the coast section. There are feral goats around the Valley; please keep your dogs under control.
Length: **3 miles/5km**; *Height Climbed:* **660ft/200m**.

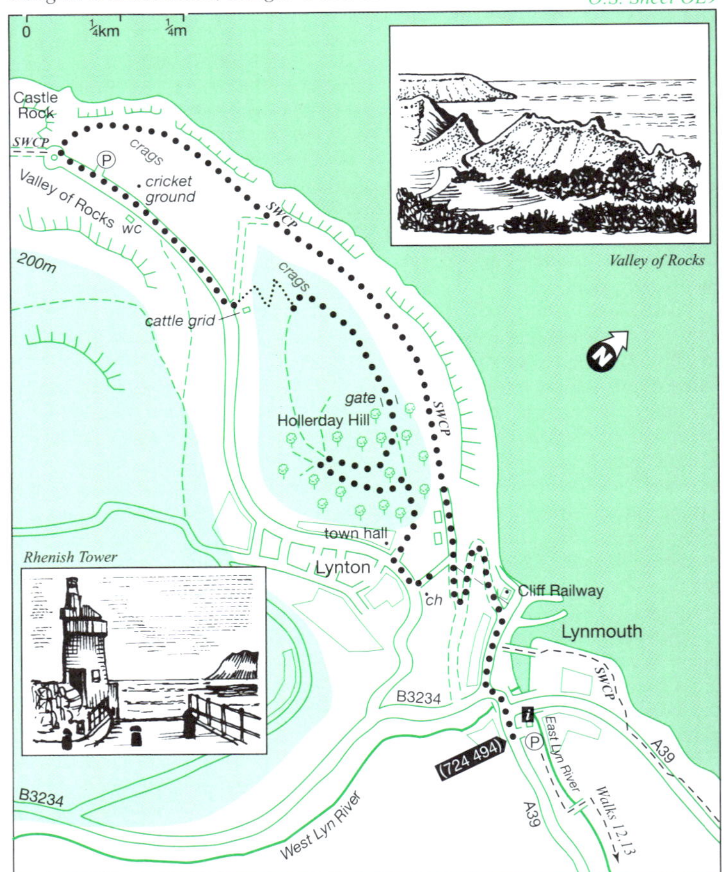

This classic walk can be started either from the car park in the Valley of Rocks or from one of the car parks at the waterfront in Lynmouth. It is described from the latter.

From the centre of Lynmouth follow the road signed for the Cliff Railway down the side of the river. The road passes a line of shops and heads towards the pier (notable for the Rhenish Tower – a splendid 19th-century folly) before swinging left. Just before it reaches the Railway (a dramatic water-powered funicular, opened in 1890, linking Lynmouth and Lynton) a sign points left for the Valley of Rocks.

Start climbing steps then join a metalled track which zig-zags up the slope, crossing and recrossing the railway. Ignore paths heading off to right and left and you climb to a junction with a road. Turn right (Valley of Rocks) and follow the road for a mile/1.6km: past hotels, out of the trees and on along the open slope above the sea. Please note that the drop is steep: care needs to be taken in windy weather.

The Valley of Rocks is a dry valley – presumably the old route of the West Lyn River – running parallel to the coast, with a line of broken crags on its northern side. The path runs along the outside of the crags until Castle Rock – the last of the crags – becomes visible ahead. The path edges left, between Castle Rock and the other crags, to join the public road at a roundabout.

Turn left along the road, passing the car park and watching out for the feral goats which inhabit the area (please keep dogs under control). Walk past the cricket ground and continue until you reach a cattle-grid with a stone pavilion up to your left just before it.

Turn back-left off the road at this point (Lynton via Hollerday Hill) – not on the tarmac track but on a grassy path climbing up and across the slope. The path zig-zags up the slope, providing the classic view of the valley as it does so, before reaching a signposted junction with a path contouring round the hill.

Either way will take you to Lynton (*see* map), but for this version of the walk go left and follow the path across the steep slope above the coast. Within a short distance the path enters woodland and reaches a kissing-gate. Immediately beyond there is a fork. The left-hand path is a short-cut, but for this walk keep right, contouring across the slope.

The path curves right to reach a grassy area with an interpretative board and a fine view. This was once the site of Hollerday House but the house was destroyed by fire in 1913 and only a few stones remain. On the far side of the site there is a signpost-ed junction. Go left (Lynton).

Within 60 paces you reach another junction. Go left again (Lynton) and follow the clear track to a hairpin bend then down the slope, through a narrow rocky defile, to enter Lynton beside the splendid Town Hall.

Turn left along the road then left again on the near side of the church to rejoin the original path.

15 Heddon's Mouth /
16 Hunters Inn to Woody Bay ___________ C/B

15) *A short walk down a narrow, wooded combe to a cliff-edged shingle beach. Length:* **2 miles/3.2km**; *Height Climbed:* **165ft/50m**. **16)** *A coastal walk on rough paths and good tracks offering wonderful views. Please note, this is a clifftop walk and should not be attempted in bad weather or by anyone nervous of heights. Length:* **6 miles/9.6km**; *Height Climbed:* **820ft/250m**.

O.S. Sheet OL9

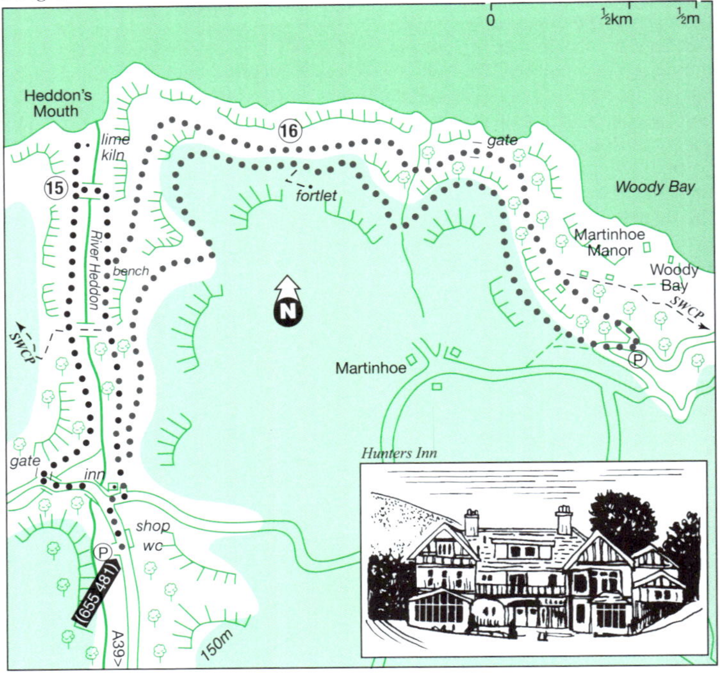

To reach the start of these two walks, drive 4 miles west from Lynton on the B3234/A39 and turn right onto the minor road for Heddon's Mouth.

It is a little over 2 miles down a narrow minor road to the car park and National Trust shop, with the splendid Hunters Inn visible beyond.

Walks 15 & 16) Walk on down the road beyond the car park. In front of the inn the road splits. Go right here, then straight away left, down a clear track, with the inn immediately to your left.

After 80 paces there is a fork. The right-hand path is the return route for Walk 16. For now, keep to the left. There is another split shortly beyond: either will do, they rejoin.

A hump-backed bridge crosses the river to your left. The Coast Path crosses here, but for these walks keep straight on. A short distance beyond there is a fork by a bench.

Walk 15) For the short walk, keep straight on (beach) down the combe. When you reach a wooden footbridge cross the river and continue down to the shingle beach, which you join just by an old lime kiln.

To complete the walk, retrace your steps to the bridge but continue beyond it with the river to your left. When you reach a signposted junction with the Coast Path keep straight on (Combe Martin). At the next junction keep straight on again (Hunters Inn) and follow the clear path to a gate onto the public road.

Turn left along the road (taking care with traffic) to return to the start.

Walk 16) For the longer walk, go right (Woody Bay), on a clear path climbing at first through scattered oak trees, then across an open slope of heather, bracken and gorse.

At the end of the first climb there is a rock jutting out to your left, which provides a great viewpoint looking along the cliffs in either direction. The path then turns to the right and climbs more gradually across the slope. This is your first glimpse of the steepness of the slope below the path: please note that it becomes even steeper further on.

The path runs along the slope then edges right, into a wooded combe. Cross the stream below a little waterfall then continue along the slope; now through woodland with wind-bent oaks arching over the path.

Go through a gate in a fence and continue. Just beyond the path turns to the right to run along the wooded slope above Woody Bay. There is no doubt about the path, which eventually joins a metalled road at the outside of a hairpin bend.

Go right (car park) and climb up to join the public road opposite a car park. Turn right along the road and you quickly reach a hairpin bend. Two signposted paths leave the road at this point. For this walk take the right-hand track (Hunters Inn).

Almost immediately a signposted footpath crosses the way. Keep straight on and follow this clear track along the top of the wood; back out of Woody Bay and on along the coast.

After a little over a mile/1.6km a sign points left for a short diversion to Martinhoe Roman Fortlet. There is little to be seen but grassy mounds but it is a fine viewpoint.

Continue along the coast and the track bends into the valley of the River Heddon and descends across the slope to return to Hunters Inn.

A complex circuit on tracks and paths, over farmland and open grazing land, passing a large natural amphitheatre. Please note that you will be passing through grazing fields – dogs must be kept under control and care taken. Length: **6 miles/9.6km**; *Height Climbed:* **720ft/220m**.

O.S. Sheet OL9

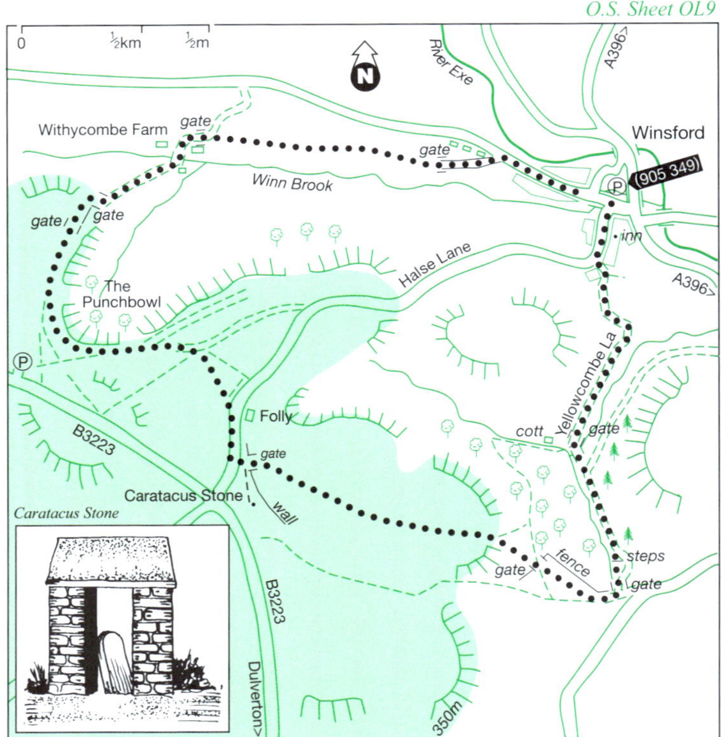

This walk can be started either from the little village of Winsford or from the car park by Winsford Hill. To find Winsford, first find the village of Dulverton (*see* Walk 20). Winsford is 5 miles north, just to the west of the A396. Winsford Hill is 2 miles south-west of the village via Halse Lane and the B3223 (*see* map). This description starts from the car park in the village.

From the centre of the village, follow the road which passes the thatched Royal Oak Inn. Start climbing out of the village. Just before the road turns hard right a sign points left for Dulverton. Walk up this clear track (Yellowcombe Lane). It splits almost immediately; keep right.

The lane climbs for a short way then descends across the slope into Yellowcombe. Just before you reach the stream there is a gate, with a cottage visible ahead-right. Go through the gate then turn left, over a stile, to reach a footbridge. Cross this and follow the path beyond (Spire Cross) to join a clear track. Turn right along this and follow it up the left-hand side of the valley.

You climb through a partly-felled conifer wood. At a sign go right, up steep steps, and follow the path up to two gates at the top of the wood. Go through the left-hand gate. You are now in a large field with no clear path. Go right, parallel to the fence to your right, to reach a gate in a line of trees, visible ahead.

At the gate there is a signpost. Go ahead-left beyond the gate (no sign), walking through open grazing land of grass, bracken and gorse. At the next signpost keep straight on (Spire Cross), crossing the highest point of the moor then keeping straight on. Looking ahead you will see an obvious house. The path takes you to a gate in a wall a little to the left of the house, on the near side of the public road.

Go through the gate. A brief diversion to the left, parallel to the wall, will lead you to the Caratacus Stone in its stone shelter (5th/6th-century; thought to commemorate a descendant of King Caratacus). Otherwise, turn right along the road.

Level with the house edge off to the left of the road. There are two grassy tracks: one running parallel to the road and the other pulling away and climbing. Take the latter.

Just short of the track's highest point there is a clear junction with a track crossing from behind-right to ahead-left. Go left and continue to the rim of The Punchbowl: a deep natural valley, wooded at its upper end.

Follow the path round the top of the valley then down the other side to reach a gate in a wall running across the slope. Go through this and continue down the right-hand side of the field beyond. At the bottom of the field there are two gates. Go through the gate to your right and join a clear track running down the slope.

The track goes through one further gate before you cross Winn Brook on a footbridge and walk up through the buildings at Withycombe Farm. Beyond the buildings, follow the access drive through a gate and turn right onto a rough path (Winsford).

Detailed description is difficult beyond this point, but there is no doubt about the route. Keep going straight ahead, through a sequence of fields, following yellow squares and arrows on the various gates. This leads to a kissing-gate with a fenced lane beyond. Follow this to the public road and turn right to return to the start.

A circuit of a large reservoir, through farmland and woodland on paths of varying quality – muddy in places. Possible link with Walk 19.
Length: **9 miles/14.4km***; Height Climbed:* undulating.

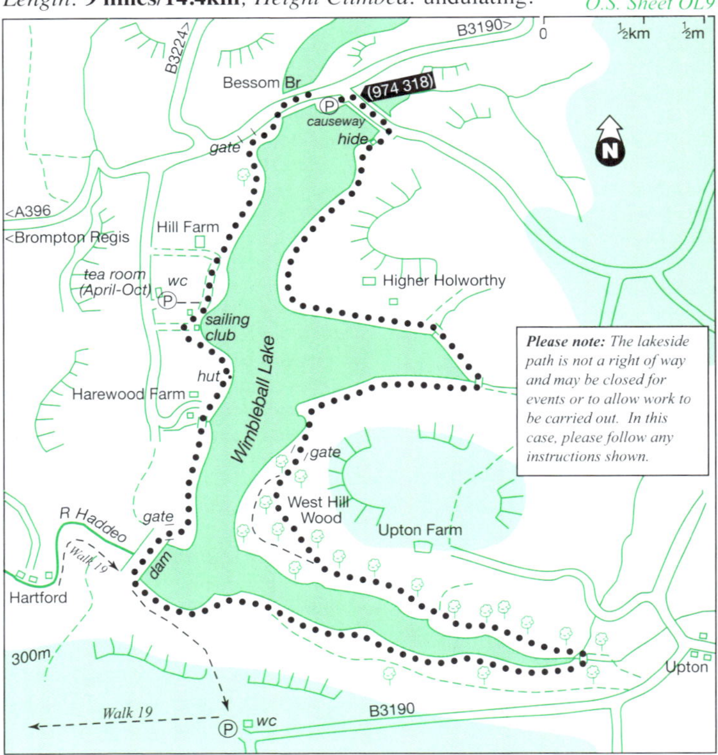

Wimbleball Lake is a large reservoir in the valley of the River Haddeo, in the south-east corner of Exmoor. A variety of watersports are carried out there – including sailing and rowing – and it is stocked for trout fishing. In addition, there is a path running right round the lake.

It is not easy to describe how to get there – follow the instructions for Walk 20, but instead of turning west for Dulverton, turn off east for the village of Brompton Regis. Follow the minor road beyond to reach Bessom Bridge and turn right just beyond (Upton). The entrance to the car park is to the right, almost immediately. (NB: for the alternative car park at the sailing club, see map.)

Walk back out of the car park and turn right along the road. After a short distance there is a small car park to the right of the road and the start of the lakeside path. Cross a small wooden bridge, pass a bird hide and continue along a clear, grassy path through a mixture of open ground and woodland.

After a mile/1.6km the path rounds a headland and runs up a deep inlet. At the head of the inlet there are footbridges/boardwalks over two streams. After the second there is a junction: go right.

Continue down the other side of the inlet and you reach a gate into West Hill Wood – a fine, mixed, broad-leaved wood. Climb for a short way beyond the gate and there is a split. The path to the right leads to a rough path by the lake; the other runs through the wood. Whichever you take they rejoin further on and continue along the narrowing reservoir.

Beyond the end of the reservoir the path continues for a short distance to reach a junction by a footbridge over a stream to your right. Go right here (dam), over the bridge.

Follow a rough footpath by the reservoir, initially through woodland and with a fence to your left, for almost 2 miles/3.2km to reach the impressive Wimbleball Dam (built 1974-8). This is the connection point with Walk 19. If you want to join that, go back-left, on a metalled road. To continue with this walk go right, over the dam.

Turn right at the far end of the dam (Harewood Farm), pass through a gate and follow the clear path beyond. You cross a footbridge over a stream just before passing below the farm, then the starting hut for the sailing races, before the path comes round a headland and the bay with the sailing club is visible ahead.

The path edges left to pass behind the boat park, passing through a gate. When you reach the entrance to the club there is a multiple junction. Go ahead-right (Bessom Bridge). That takes you across the entrance road and through a gate at the top of a clear track, with a playground to your left.

The track passes the rowing club shed and continues round the bay until it goes through a gate, beyond which it edges away from the water. Follow this up to a further gateway. Immediately beyond this the metalled track goes left, past the buildings at Hill Farm, but you keep straight on along a rougher track (Bessom Bridge).

Follow the lakeside path up to a gate leading on to a quiet public road. Don't go through the gate; turn right on the near side and follow a path with the fence to the left to reach the start of Bessom Bridge.

Cross the bridge (there is a pavement). At the far end there is a stile to the right of the road, leading into the grassy area below the car park.

19 Haddon Hill & Bury ____________________ A

A complex circuit through woodland, farmland and open moorland, following clear tracks, rough paths and a section of quiet public road. Please note that Haddon Lane can be very wet. National Park leaflet available. Length: **6 miles/9.5km***; Height Climbed:* **660ft/200m***. Possible link with Walk 18.*

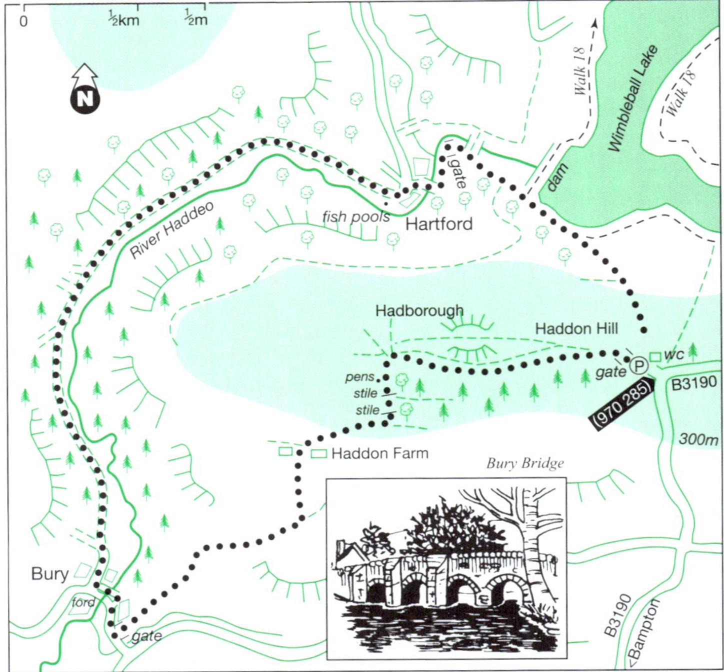

The start of this walk is at the car park for Haddon Hill, just south of Wimbleball Lake (*see* Walk 18) in the south-east corner of Exmoor. Access to the car park is off the B3190 road, which links Watchet and Bampton.

The car park is approximately 4 miles north of Bampton.

Walk to the corner of the car park furthest from the entrance road and go through a gate on a good track. The track splits immediately. Keep left, with a strip of moorland to your left and pine trees beyond.

The path climbs gradually, through grass, bracken and gorse, then – once the high point of Hadborough is passed to your right – descends to a complex junction. Go sharp left, towards scattered trees beyond the main plantation.

The path passes immediately to the left of the pony pens to reach a stile on the edge of a wooded area. Immediately beyond the stile a clear track heads off to the left. Ignore this and keep straight on, along a fainter path heading downhill near the right-hand edge of the trees.

After a short distance you reach a stile over a fence. Cross this and turn right along the lane beyond. This weaves left then right (ignore the track coming in from behind-left). Bear right on the track which then runs straight to reach the buildings at Haddon Farm.

Walk past the back of the farmhouse then edge half-left (Bury). This leads you to the top of a deep lane. Follow this lane downhill for a mile/1.6km. Views open up in places, but please note that the lane is muddy at the best of times, and can be very wet when it has been raining.

At the foot of the lane you go through a gate and enter the hamlet of Bury between houses. Turn right along the road to reach the old bridge by the ford over the River Haddeo. Cross this. Beyond the bridge the road splits: go right.

In a short distance the road ends. Level with the last house to the right there is a signposted junction. Go straight on (Hartford) along a clear track. You will be following this pleasant track through mixed woodland for the next 2 miles/3.2km. A number of tracks and paths head off to right and left; just aim to stay on the clear track nearest the left-hand side of the River Haddeo.

At the far end of the track you pass a series of fish pools then enter the buildings in the hamlet of Hartford. At a signposted junction go right (Upton). You immediately reach another junction. Go ahead-left between fences (Upton). This brings you to the river. Go left for a few paces to reach a footbridge. Cross this and turn left at the far end.

You start along a track which becomes a grassy path which soon joins a metalled road at an angle (blue marker post). Go ahead-right along this (Upton). Pass through a gate by a cattle-grid, keep right at the fork shortly beyond and follow the road steeply uphill to reach the end of the dam at Wimbleball Lake.

A turn to the left at this point (over the dam) links with Walk 18. For this route, however, just keep straight on. The road continues climbing, through woodland at first, and quickly reaches a signposted junction. The bridleway for Upton heads off ahead-left, but for this walk keep straight on along the metalled road.

A track comes in from behind-right. Ignore this and continue. When the road begins to level out you will see the car park across the rough ground to your right.

A circuit on clear tracks (and a short stretch of road) by a river and through woods and farmland, including one steep climb. Length: **4 miles/6.4km**; *Height Climbed:* **460ft/140m**.

Dulverton is a pleasant village on the south-east corner of Exmoor, about 17 miles south of Minehead via Dunster and the A396. Park in the car park in the centre of the village, walk back out of the entrance and turn left.

Walk down the street to reach the road bridge over the River Barle. At the far end turn right, up Oldberry Lane. When the road splits, at some houses, keep right. There are two further splits just beyond: keep right at both (for Hawkridge, at the second).

Ignore a path going left for the Middle Path (an alternative route through the woods) and continue – sometimes by the river and sometimes with fields to your right. After a mile/1.6km the path passes through two gates amongst the buildings at Kennel Farm to reach the public road.

Follow this quiet road (with care) to Marsh Bridge and walk back over the river. On the far side you will see an old packhorse bridge down to your right.

There is a flurry of road junctions beyond the bridge. As the road bends right, take the second road off to the left. This quickly climbs to a T-junction with another road. Go straight across this and walk up a clear track (Court Down).

After a short distance a second track comes in from behind-right. Ignore this and continue climb-

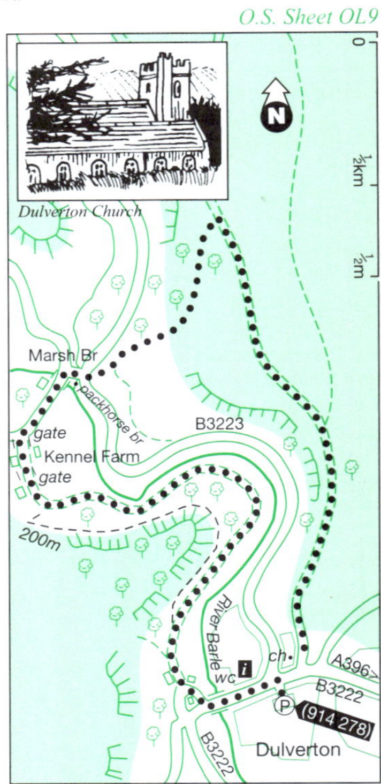

ing. After climbing steeply for ½ mile/0.8km you reach a signposted junction with a clear track. Turn right here (Dulverton) and follow the track for a little over a mile/1.6km to return to the start, entering Dulverton behind the handsome church.